TRIUMPH HOUSE

INSPIRATIONS

Edited by Chris Walton

First published in Great Britain in 1996 by
TRIUMPH HOUSE
1 - 2 Wainman Road, Woodston,
Peterborough, PE2 7BU

HB ISBN 1 86161 018 1
SB ISBN 1 86161 013 0

Foreword

Inspirations is a wonderful anthology of poetry that contains the thoughts, feelings and emotions of over 140 new and established poets.

Each holds the special gift of being able to set a scene, share a story, and pass on a message through their writing.

Faith, hope, and love are just a few of the many subjects chosen by the writers. Together they have created a collection of some of the most inspirational Christian poetry that is being written today.

Chris Walton
Editor

CONTENTS

GOD'S PAIN

I was out walking one day
I heard God say
I ask you to help me Son.
I want you to let me tell you and show you my kingdom,
I am everywhere
I look and stare
I am a tree
I have scum on my bark you see.
I also am the grass and soil.
I feel tired from what man's done with his greed and toil.
I cannot breath, the air is not clean,
I know in people this can be seen.
I should be blue and white in the sky,
I know I am dirty with a shade of grey, how I cry.
I love the people so,
I see lots ill and suffer slow.
I mix with animals and birds.
I look at them they tell me I don't feel right but don't use words.
I see, yes the sea.
I talk to fish, they are me and slowly dying you see.
I ask you again,
I am your God, clean me and free me of pain.

Robert John Quinlan

THE GRADUATE

Sophisticated mind somehow speak up
Acknowledge the purpose of life.
As silent waves of sentiment do pause -
Masterful but inconclusive,
Ravenous until antique -
Answerable to anonymous vogue
Tender are thy feet . . .
As anniversary of time wages war,
The gates of truth conclude.
There's life beyond the physical
Uncertainty is removed.

Pat Woods

HE TOLD ME SO

There are many things I do not know or even understand,
But I know my Father holds me in His ever loving hand.
My Father loves me as I am, I know, he told me so,
I also know He's changing me, of this I am now sure.
When I call on Him for help, I'm sure that He is there.
I know it's true, He told me so - He listens to my prayer.
When I'm feeling lonely, I know that He's with me -
I turn to Him for comfort and the love that sets me free.
I know that God is with me wherever I may go -
I know it's true, it has to be, because *He* told me so.

Sandra Barker

NEVER ALONE

You are never alone
I am never alone
We are never alone
Thanks to God on high.

He sent us His love in the shape of His Son
To show us how life is to be
Give your life to me
and I will show you how it will be.

My life is nothing without Him
My life would be nothing at all
without his love and forgiveness
Making sense of my life overall.

If you are lonely and feeling that no-body cares
then think of what God has given to you.
The pain and suffering He endured
Just for you.

Pamela Buxton

SPRING

Flowers are opening up their buds,
Leaves are on the tree.
Lambs are leaping in the field,
Such wonderful sights to see.

Everywhere you look around,
Throughout the whole wide earth.
Really beautiful things to see,
Spring is the time of new birth.

These things were made by God's own hand,
Father of all around we see.
And when the season of spring is here,
Earth is a wonderful place to be.

Christina Staff

RAINBOW

See the rainbow's grand extent,
Through the rain mist gently bent.
Never varied colours bright,
Diadem of tinted light.

Each hue in its appointed place,
God's promise to the human race.
That never shall we see again,
Forty days of flooding rain.

Some wise men say that this attraction,
Is prismatic light refraction.
But I prefer the grand concept,
That the rainbow is a promise kept.

Arthur Haskell

RESURRECTION

I stood in my garden one autumn morning,
Just as the cold grey light was dawning.
The leaves from the trees on the ground lay dead,
My once brilliant flowers - their colour now fled -
were folding their leaves for the winter ahead.
Snow came with the winter and covered the ground,
No leaf from the tree and no flower was found.
But beneath the snow in the cold hard sod,
The roots would respond to the call of God.
To wake again into bud and leaf,
After the winter's long sleep.
When springtime came, where the dead leaf had been -
The tree had a bud then a leaf of green.
The flowers through winter asleep neath the snow,
Came to life in the lovely bright colours I know.

Is nature a parable? Proving the word,
Spoken by Jesus to people who heard -
him call from the dead Lazarus His friend,
This wonderful miracle was not the end.
For Jesus said, 'All who in death's sleep do lay
shall hear me call them to life in that day.'
He went to the grave and our ransom He paid,
Then risen from death this promise He made.
'I will return, God's kingdom will come -
the dead in that day shall rise from the tomb.'
When the autumn of life and its winter is past,
God's springtime will bring new life that will last.
The Lord will be King of the earth in that day,
Death will be ended and *Love* crown the way.

Gladys Morte

THE TRANSFIGURATION

A man who once had seemed like any other -
Was veiled in dazzling light and shimmering haze.
The Lord of Life in robes of glistening whiteness,
Through time and space transcended - to amaze
His friends, who watched in fearful trepidation
That glimpse of Heavenly glory, yet to be.
Unable to define an earthly meaning,
They gazed in wonder - lost in ecstasy.

Transfigured there upon the glowing mountain,
With Moses and Elijah by His side
Stood Jesus, in a shining light of splendour,
Appraised by God, His Spirit glorified.
We may not understand the Vision's meaning,
But if on earth the love of God we see.
Time will reveal the radiance and the beauty,
Within that perfect life - eternally.

Joan Vergette Goodman

YOU ARE THERE

In the restless streets and houses
and the solitude of peace.
In the chaos of humanity
You are there.

In the smile of reassurance
and the mind that's full of doubt.
In the warm of embrace of loving arms
You are there.

In the elderly full of wisdom
and the innocence of a child.
In the recklessness of youthful ways
You are there.

In the stillness of a balmy night
and the bustle of the day.
In the beauty of creation
You are there.

In the news that brings good tidings
and a problem that's been solved.
In a wound where pain is healing
You are there.

In the breaking down of barriers
and in bridges that are built.
In the love of all your people
You are there.

Anne P Ainley

WALKING ON AIR

They seem to walk and run on air
this 'joy of living,' laughing pair.
As hand in hand they keep in touch
with all they see and like so much.
These walks become the prayers they pray
and cares and worries melt away.

With swinging arms and carefree stride,
they walk where mutual feelings bide,
in ev'ry view towards the sea,
in ev'ry cliff top flow'r and tree.
In sea birds as they feed or fly,
and Skylarks singing songs on high.

In vantage points inspiring thought,
in ev'ry lesson clearly taught,
by God in much which they behold,
where beauty doth in arms enfold,
all those who feel their spirits rise,
and earthly man is heav'nly wise.

They love the changes which appear,
in seasons, four of ev'ry year.
The rising and the setting sun,
the stars that shine when day is done.
The dark clouds racing by the moon,
the pink tipped clouds of afternoon.

Most ev'rything they see they love,
from sea below to sky above,
and slowly, almost unaware,
a love is born which they will share,
this 'Joy of Living', laughing pair,
who seem to walk and run on air.

W P Gill

UNTITLED

With a formless mass, God made His mark,
Out of naught He brought forth light and dark.
The moon by night the sun by day,
And all creation beneath God's sway.

God smiled from Heaven and said, 'It's good'
Every animal, plant, tree and bud.
Man He created over all
But too soon He let God's standards fall.

The earth is spoiled by man's pollution
Only God has the solution.
But man his back on God has turned
The command 'to care' for all things has been spurned.

Lord open our eyes to see anew,
Let Your beautiful creation be our view.
Let us hear again Your words to creation,
God say, 'It's good *this* world *this* nation.'

Animals, birds, trees and seed,
Man of every colour and creed.
Lift up your hearts to God above,
Who gave us this earth, a labour of love.

Denise Helsby

THOUGHTS ON A WINTER'S DAY

The day is cold, the air is crisp, the ground
Covered by a blanket of white, lies hidden
'Neath winters cloak of dazzling snow.
No sound or movement gives away the secret
Of the life that lies below this warming shawl.
        Grumbles and groans are all the tones,
        Which issue from the mouths of men.
        Frozen pipes and chilly bones,
        Power cuts and train delays.
        Endless coughs and colds and moans,
        Lasting throughout many days.
But stop awhile and think more cheerfully
Winter cold foretells a springtime bright.
In God's good time the snow will disappear
Revealing once again new life of colour,
Warmth and beauty. Snowdrops delicately formed
And crocuses, bring colour to the scene.
And later, as the sun brings greater warmth
The primrose enters to enrich our eyes.
Spring calls us out to wander through her home,
The countryside of lane and forest glade,
Admiring all the growth and new life shown.
Without the winter months, which must come first
Spring would not so glorious seem. The plan
Of life is wonderfully shaped to keep
Us ever looking forward. And so we find
New hope in winter's cold, and comfort too -
In the poet's words -
'If winter comes, can spring be far behind?'

Jean Hill

SPRING PRAYER

A wayside tractor, laborious in sound
Awakes hibernating senses too long deeply bound.
Here is God's goodness, the bursting of Spring,
And a Wonder of *All* such a season can bring.

Sight is bombarded, a rainbow of hues,
So much to take in, such wondrous views.
Let's generously acknowledge this breath-taking creation,
Surely existing throughout each nation.

Daffodils of lemon fields of grassy green,
Snowy, fragrant blossoms, the most glorious seen.
Drooping, shy snowdrops, hyacinths of spectrum blue,
And the feathery fragility of encrusted webs with dew.

A symphonic poem of blue-tit chatter,
Complaining blackbirds and magpie clatter.
Fun-loving squirrels chasing and leaping,
And new-born lambs nuzzlingly feeding.

Grant us Lord the gift of appreciation,
Avoiding damage, destruction and all desecration.
Help us to cherish each gift of Thine,
Now and forever, till the end of Time.

Elizabeth Ness

LAKELAND BEAUTY

Mountains proud, rugged and majestic
Dominate the horizon in beauty fantastic.
Guardian parents of meadows below,
Gathering clouds and vapours that flow.
Watering the meadows lying in their laps,
Luscious green aprons filled with sap.
Mirroring lakes and streams filling the gaps,
We gasp with wonder at their beauty.
As mountains harmoniously do their duty,
Do they lose their patience we wonder?
When crags and peaks echo with thunder.
When rain, snow, wind lash into their side,
Making earth and rocks to slide.
No, they sit enthroned in majestic beauty,
Calm and patient doing their duty,
Teaching us lessons of permanent love.
Firm and solid forever stood,
Like their Creator in Heaven above.

Fred Sidaway

A THOUGHT

I lie awake and watch the moon,
Up there so high.
And in the day the sun shines down
From the blue sky.

Sometimes I think of mighty things,
Like roaring seas.
Of sandy deserts, mountain tops
And forest trees.

Among all these I often feel,
So very small.
I wonder God should even notice
Me at all!

But Jesus said He sees each bird,
Fall from a tree.
And so I know, that though a child
He must know me.

K Greenall

A PRAYER FOR A CHILD

Light four candles for a child
At the corner of his bed.
Four apostles keeping watch
At the foot and at his head.

Ask the Holy Trinity
For their everlasting light.
Pray that every day may bring,
Threefold graces fair and bright.

Sun and moon shine down on him,
Stars surround his sleeping frame.
When he wakes the sun shall shine,
Each and every day the same.

Give this child a simple soul,
Singleness of heart and mind.
One life to live, one heart to give,
One love until the end of time.

Joan Tyack

EASTER WEEK

Holy week has come again,
For us to celebrate.
Maundy Thursday - food of life,
Given to commemorate.
Good Friday on our sins we dwell,
For these our Jesus died.
Saturday empty and forlorn
The apostles tried to hide,
But Easter morn all gloom dispelled,
With our God's approbation.
Christ had risen from the tomb
And proved to every nation
He was truly Son of God.
Our Master, Lord and King.
The Scripture had then been fulfilled -
Hosannas; Hallelujahs sing!

Elizabeth Hunter

BELIEVE AND TRUST

God spoke to me this morning at the breaking of the day,
Through the radiance of a sunrise with its life sustaining rays.
He was present in the birdsong, the flowers and the trees,
'Just trust in me,' he seemed to say, 'I will provide your needs.'

Man spoke to me this morning, through the horror of the news,
With tales of rape and murder, muggings and war crimes too.
It spoke of man's inhumanity to man, of burglaries, thefts and greed,
Of those who deal in drugs and porn, of an evil, wicked creed.

Christ spoke to me this morning through those who love and care,
For even in earth's darkest spots His love is everywhere.
'Believe in me, have no fear tho' the way be dark and grim,
For I have gone before you, I have conquered death and sin.'

Malcom F Andrews

FORGIVENESS

Have you forgiven 'so and so?' I used to ask,
With little experience of such things myself.
But everyone knows Jesus' teaching on forgiveness,
And from the cross, His words:
'Father, forgive them, for they know not what they do.'
Yes, of course we know them,
In theory, at least!

But to forgive in practice,
Those great hurts we've received ourselves,
Can be a very different matter.

'Oh yes Lord, I have forgiven them, I'm sure.'
 - Then why is it, that I hear myself say inwardly:
'I'm not going to stand for that!'
And later too, 'I'm just not going to stand for it.'
 - That doesn't sound like forgiveness, does it?
And a great cloud of gloom seems to settle over me . . .

'O Lord, how can I freely forgive this hurt, unconditionally?'
Then I remember that boy's father's words to Jesus:
'I believe; help thou my unbelief.'   (Mark ch.9:24)
And so I pray, 'I forgive, but help Thou, my unforgiving too.'
Then - a miracle - the cloud lifted - the sun shone,
And I was new!
But amazing grace - a second miracle was due.

Minutes later, my son announced, 'There's someone here for you.'
Quite surprised, I look; and can't believe it's true.
That very same one said: 'I've come to apologise to you!'
. . . What joy was there in our embrace . . .
      A sign of Love from Our Lord's grace!

Anne Boddy

PIPE DREAMS

God's smiling down from His Heaven,
At last there is peace on the earth.
No more are there warring factions,
Just contentment and joy and mirth.

No nation's in need or starving,
For countries who have the most share.
At last people have come to their senses,
They've learnt how to comfort and care.

The animal Kingdom is thriving,
Even though greed did its worst.
To drive wild life to extinction,
Yet the animals lived here first.

What a wonderful dream someone's having,
If all this we could only provoke.
It seems someone's been chasing the dragon,
And pipe-dreams disappear with the smoke.

Bell Ferris

UNTITLED

I went into the church and it was dark and cold,
Candles burned and windows coloured light.
It was very beautiful and very, very old.
God was not there.
The door was open and I walked out into the wood,
The leaf-light covered me.
The breeze, the woods, the ferns,
The ground and downwards to the sea,
The ripple-light, the sky and God was there.

Alison Jacobs

LOOK LORD!

See the tiny infant
gently held in mother's arms.
look in love upon him Jesus
keep him safe from harm.

See he grasps a finger,
warm security he knows,
put your arms of love around him
securely, as he grows.

See his eyes wide open,
the whole wide world to view,
through all the business of life
Lord, may he see you.

See, we welcome the baby
surround him with the prayer
that you will love and keep him
always in your care.

Joan Miles Lister

MINE

My substitute, my died in place
My bringer of eternal grace
My hand of God, my judgement fire
My soother of the Father's ire
My Heavenly day, my sweetest sound
My caller of the lost and found
My hurting Christ, my crucified
My sorrow, broken heart, who died
My feet, my nails, my hands broke bare
My hill, my cross was lifted there
My heart, my dreadful heart, my sin
My two-torn veil, my entrance in
My God, eternal glory, home
My truth, my crown, no more alone.

Lee Morris

GOD'S GARDEN

Folk resemble garden flowers,
Each needing special care.
Some flourish in the noon day sun,
While others wither there.

Now take the friendly *Rambling Rose,*
She needs gentle pruning,
While the stately *Canterbury Bell,*
May now and then need tuning.

The modest little *Violet*,
Would rather hide her face.
Than be a *Flowering Climber*,
She could never stand the pace.

We must be careful how we treat,
Each other on life's way.
And in God's garden take our place,
Contented there to stay.

Mary Peagram

MY SIMPLE RELIGION

Faith is God's second gift,
To all mankind.
His first, is life itself,
Faith is believing.
Without seeing
Without proof.
It is the everlasting power
To sustain us.
Through tragedy, disaster,
The death of those we love.
And, if at times,
We lose our faith
The world grows
Bleak and cold.
We question - Why?
We cannot see beyond the day.
Have lost our faith
The faith that lights
The darkest path.
The hand that leads us on
To overcome each obstacle.
Achieving joy beyond imagination.
Hold to your faith,
Hold to your dream.
If it's right for you,
It will come true.
Have faith in God,
He has His faith in you.

Thomas C Rymarsh

WHAT GIVES US THE RIGHT?

What gives us the right
To sit in judgement on our fellow man?
Who decides what is right or wrong
What we can't do or what we can?

Moses descended from the mountain
Carrying tablets made of stone.
Etched with God's laws we should obey,
Or so the Bible made it known.

But were those Ten Commandments
Moses personal biased way,
Of trying to make His fellow man
Believe that to Him God did say.

Take these tablets from the mountain
To those sinners down below.
And you strike fear deep in their hearts,
The power of the true God let them know.

But why did God speak to just one man?
Why not to them all?
Why did he not show His awesome power
In an act to make man crawl?

John the Baptist, Moses, Jesus
Napoleon, Hitler, Attilla the Hun.
Supposedly good and bad men,
Caused equal amounts of the deaths to come.

Only I am the true Disciple,
And my destiny fulfilled when
I finally decide there is a God,
And He will know and say, Amen.

Don Woods

'TWAS GOD

Who put the myriad stars into space,
And gave the sun and moon their face?
Who divided the night from day,
And made this world in splendid array?

Who made the mountains, majestic and steep,
And clothed the valleys with grazing sheep?
Who made the lakes, the rivers and streams,
Clefts in the rock and mighty ravines?

Who made the rain to fall to the ground,
The crash of thunder and the lightening come down?
Who made the snowflakes so white and small,
Each tiny one different as they fall?

Who made the spider with its intricate web,
The honey bees as the queen they fed?
Who made the eagle to soar on its wings,
The nightingale, as its little voice sings?

Who made the trees in the forest so grand,
And who can number the grains of sand?
Who made the flowers, their perfume so sweet,
Seed time and harvest as we gather wheat?

Who placed the seed in that mother so mild,
And brought forth Jesus - the Holy Christ Child?
Who rejected the precious Son of Man,
That we might be saved through the blood of the Lamb?
'Twas God.

Diane Mary Watt

MY BIBLE

Each day I put some time aside
When I read the word of God.
A corner of the afternoon
With a book about my Lord.

My worries and my cares I take
And put all to one side.
Then read of when Jesus walked
Upon this world of mine.

This special book tells to me,
The miracle of His birth.
And how He blessed and healed the poor,
And He walked upon the earth.

His miracles are there to see,
On each and every page.
And how He preached of love to all,
And then He was betrayed.

It tells how men told many lies,
Then nailed Him to a tree.
And how He rose to be with God
That we may all be free.

The life of Jesus is written down
On pages edged with gold.
So everyone can know His word,
In a book that never grows old.

G Mullett

REBIRTH

When these old mortal bones of mine have crumbled into dust,
Let my Spirit rise to find another place.
Somewhere beyond our puny world, where I can re-adjust,
And fly into the vaulted halls of space.

When I was young I used to lie on earth's sweet grassy bed,
To watch the clouds above go skimming by.
Considering the mysteries of what may be ahead,
When I approach the portals of the sky.

Imagination leads me on, I tread the milkyway,
Surrounded by a million diamond stars.
Then sped around *Diana's* moon, to greet a brand new day,
And marvel at the rosy orb of *Mars!*

Still further on I gaze in awe, on *Saturn's* coloured rings,
And hope that this is Heavens door.
I watch the silver spears go by which great *Orion* flings,
And wish my quest might last forevermore.

Such wonders fill the firmament, beyond the ken of man,
Bright *Venus* now shows her shining face.
Each awesome spectacle, all working to the plan,
Created and ordained by God's good grace!

L Muscroft

CALM IN THE STORM

All over the world men's hearts fail with fear,
Fear of the present, fear for the future.
Dangers abound everywhere,
Rulers deposed, sometimes killed without warning.
No time to choose then twixt evil and good,
Oh! . . . if only today people would
Come and acknowledge there's one overall.
One day before Him we all must fall,
Then - will we greet Him with joy in our heart,
Or will we hear those words, ' Depart
I never knew you,' sad, sad the day.
If from our Saviour we turn away,
Following after the tinsel and gloss.
Find at the end - nothing but dross.
Nothing that lasts for eternity
Nothing to bring when His face we see,
Nothing to lay at His feet.
Today He is seeking, to Him we are dear,
As Shepherd He calls us to follow Him here.
Then we shall know, whatever betide,
Always a friend is there at our side.
Dangers and sorrows may come to us still,
But when we trust then we know He will
Hold us fast in His mighty hand,
Safely we'll reach the Promised Land.
There to behold Him, with joy to say
Thank you for guiding us all the way

Kay Wythe

GARDEN OF EDEN

Things in the garden look lovely,
As Adam sat there with Eve.
Naming the plants and the flowers,
And even the birds in the trees.
When down slithered Satan the devil,
When Adam had just slipped away.
Is it true that the fruit from the garden
Has been forbidden to you from this day?
'No' from the fruit of the garden we can eat it,
But as the tree that gives knowledge and life,
We must not touch or eat it or in that day we will die.
'No' that's not true said the devil,
In that day you'll know goodness from bad,
And Eve, she listened to the devil.
And the future for them now was sad,
They were driven right out of the garden.
To a world full of thistles and strife,
And that's how sin got started.
All through Adam and his wife.
But God Has sent us a Saviour,
Christ Jesus is His name.
Through Him we can find a future,
And paradise regained.

M Kay

YOU GAVE ME A BEAUTIFUL DAY LORD

You gave me a beautiful day Lord
And what did I do?
I just abused it - when I could have used it
To glorify you.
The sound of the birdsong - those beautiful flowers,
Were not heard or noticed in my wasted hours.
Precious moments I just spoilt by angry thoughts inside,
Feelings of bitterness and hate I really could not hide.
I heard somebody shout your name - but they used it just to swear,
And although I thought it was a shame - I did not really care.

You have me a beautiful day Lord
And what did I do?
I did not abuse it - I really did use it
To glorify you.
The children were laughing - the day was so bright,
I counted my blessings from morning till night.
Precious moments I enjoyed my heart was glad and free,
I felt such happiness inside because you cared for me.
I told somebody of your love - they heard what I had to say,
It just seemed the right thing to do - on such a lovely day . . .

Val Furbank

HEAVEN IS

Heaven is but a state of mind,
When thoughts within there are all kind.
Where love transcends all of the hate,
And joy and happiness perpetuate.
Where all the dull days show up bright,
And rain drops shine like stars at night,
Where soft white clouds go sailing by
On a lake of blue that is the sky.
Where rivers of silver gently wend,
From mountains high to their journey's end
Where trees spread out their leafy arms.
Enhancing nature and all her charms,
Where butterflies dance in the breeze.
Sweet minutes to watch and please,
Where all animals have a chance to roam.
On this earth of ours we call home,
Where the waters of the seas ebb and flow.
Carrying ships of love as their main cargo,
Where all mankind can live in peace.
And the joys of living never cease
Then we could reach a peace of mind,
The nearest Heaven, on earth you will find.

Frederick Jolly

LIFE EVER-LASTING

Life to life Jesus came to give,
Now our future's sure we will live.
By the grace of God, He was born,
So the world would know of Christmas morn.
Good news came to all the earth,
With this amazing Holy Birth.
Let all bells ring and people sing,
The Lord above be praised.
By this act of God and His Love,
Jesus Christ from death was raised.
To be a guide and show the way,
Everlasting life is here to stay.

Barbara Smith

WHERE DOST THOU TAKE ME AT NIGHT LORD?

Restless lonely people in the night,
Search for comfort, from a distance.
Lives so incomplete without the light,
Praying humbly for assistance.
The bed is a desert or a deep dark ocean,
Constantly still, showing no emotion.
They hug their pillows as they sail through time,
This is their private world and also mine.

Sad tunes played on heart strings as they ride,
Endless journey, no direction.
Melting like a candle from inside,
Adding lessons to their collection.
On dream's magic carpet, no compass on the bow.
Destiny planned but they don't know how.
Cruising through back streets, where love is a crime,
This is their private world and also mine.

Steer me a course I can fly on,
I know you are a pilot I can rely on.
I leave it all up to you, I don't care just how far,
Please make this a good trip whoever you are.

End of escape here comes the day,
Endless cycle, to rely on.
I really would have liked a longer stay,
I found a shoulder I could cry on.
I wish the day away for escape to return,
The day is for living, the night time to learn.
Wasting away the hours for that midnight chime,
This is my private world, and it's all mine.

Bill Jones

THE LOVE OF GOD

Long ago by God's word
The heaven's and earth were born.
From water and by water
By God's almighty hand.
These creations that you see,
And smell and touch and breathe.
These creations from above,
Were created for us with love.
Do not worry about your life,
What you will eat or drink.
Or expensive clothes that you want to wear,
Life is more precious than these.
We are here by God's love,
So make an ambition to lead a quiet life.
To work with your hands
Earn an honest living.
And win the respect you deserve,
Are we ever content with what we have
And does greed step in?
Just remember we were born with nothing,
And take nothing when we leave.
Do not merely listen to the teaching of God's word,
For God showed His love to us,
By sending His only Son.
Jesus gave His life for us,
In the hope that we would gain wisdom.
So when it is time to leave this world,
We can live within His kingdom.

J Williams

THE POWER OF PRAYER

Have you ever needed someone, and you find no-one there?
People don't want to listen, they don't seem to care,
You feel depressed, and you're really feeling down,
Nights enfold you, with her black velvet gown.

You lie awake, wondering, what can you do.
What will the next day bring forth for you?
It's then you may think, perhaps you should pray,
To ask God for help, to show you the way.

We all at some stage, need a really good friend.
Someone we can rely on, on who we can depend.
Perhaps you may think, that no-one can help,
You feel miserable, and sorry for yourself.

No-one knows how God really works.
But we know, He takes away fears, and soothes away hurt.
God is all around, He can be anywhere,
But He will always listen, and He'll always care.

Miracles can happen, even in these days.
God carries them out, in lots of different ways.
You don't have to be in Church, or Chapel, to speak to Him,
When you've hurt someone, or even committed a sin.

All He asks for, is that you show regret, and some remorse.
Perhaps you lost your temper, there was no justifiable cause.
There is simply nothing, you cannot tell God in Prayer.
You should know that He loves you, that He will always care.

The 'Power of Prayer' can do so much good.
God answers our Prayers, in the way that only He could.
You may not agree, perhaps with God's method or choice,
But you have the proof, that God listened, and He heard your voice.

R Chamberlain

WOULDN'T IT BE HEAVEN IF . . .

To each his own heaven - a longing indeed,
What must be to assuage the present need.
So it has been the ages through;
Heaven to the ancients was the best they knew.
Israelites parched by wind and sand
Sought the shade of a rock in a weary land.
Greeks of old saw, in their dreams,
Elysian fields watered by flowing streams.
Nordic warriors who never would yield,
Borne by winged Valkyrie from brave battlefield.
Heaven for the sick, relief from pain,
For maimed and crippled, to leap again;
For those who are blind, new eyes to see,
For the caged and imprisoned - oh to be free!
For those who see loneliness years without end,
Warmth, companionship and love of a friend.
What was your heaven, Christ, dying tormented, alone?
Did you yearn for your Father, your loved and your own?
To leave this sad weary world of men
Who had hurt and denied you again and again?
Or did you know as we know now, that when you pierce the great divide,
All those lovely earthly things must be left on the other side?
Did you look back fondly to the parties, wine and laughter,
All the human joys with no part in the hereafter?
Did you see again the hillsides, bright with carpets of flowers,
Or recall the scent of fields moistened by summer showers?
Did you remember the workshop, 'Work the way of the grain,'
As you stood in the fragrant shavings that curled away from the plane?
The fires you lit on the seashore as you waited and watched the dawn come,
Blue smoke spiralling upward to welcome the fishing boats home;
The rush and roar of the tempest sweeping the quiet sea,
All the blessed memories of a lifetime in Galilee.

Did you think of this when you said,
'What greater love, what higher price,
To surrender it all for another,
The ultimate sacrifice?'

Marie Roberts

HOW MUCH

Religion. Belief or truth.
Science. Fact or fiction.
A battle between the two in the world arena.
Turin shroud becomes the dishcloth of the scientist.
Genesis begins time what about the dinosaurs.
One side big bang, one side God's power.
Miracles are just party tricks, Chinese whispers.
Who do you believe, take the plunge pick a side
Science ridicules religion, no equations, no facts.

Religion smothers progress, Darwinism suppressed by churches.
Court case over evolution, the judge will decide.
Money is the root of all evil,
Give generously to the collection plate.
Holy war fought on unholy terms.
Death to the unbeliever, thou shalt not kill.
Vatican city, spiritual capital.
Greed and poverty lives next door.
Religion hates science, questions the creator.
This world isn't big enough for the both of them.
Numbers dwindle, church pews empty.
Worried, yes the collection plates empty too.
Save your soul for a price
How much.

Jonas

UNDERSTANDING

They said she was patient
They said she was kind
They said she had great understanding.

She, chained to a wheelchair,
Always in pain,
Listened to everyone's trouble.

They said she was brave
They said she was great,
But they hadn't got her understanding.

She suffered without any grumbles,
Without ever making a moan,
Till God showed her His understanding
And took her joyously home.

Twinks Perugini Kenyon

A GIFT FROM GOD

The golden sun shines down below
It fills me with an inner glow,
I look up at the clear blue sky
You can see the sparkle in my eye.

Summer breezes billow by
Enfolding me like a shawl.
The grass so green, each blade so neat,
I'm overcome with awe.

As I touch the petal of a rose,
Its dew falls like a tear;
A cloud floats by in the clear blue sky
And the cause of these feelings are clear.

Gifts like these are for all to see
But I have an extra joy;
God smiled at me, He gave to me
The love of a single boy!

Jayne Hilary Lowry

CREATION AND DESTINATION

The conception of creation
from earth's first early dawn,
believers and non-believers
pondered since they were born.
Not science nor anthropology
have really satisfied,
the ultimate or absolute
however hard they've tried.
While birth and death are visible,
we know how they arrive,
but after death - the mystery,
what is there to survive?
There are those who claim some knowledge,
but can they show some proof?
Until in turn, we reach our end,
how can we know the truth?
Is it all a big illusion,
that truth towards which we grope?
Christians prefer to live by faith
and in that faith to hope.

Joyce Higgs

THE TRIO

Three little girls, each eight years old, had a chat in the schoolyard,
one day;
Lucy was British, Suzie Chinese and African, Ellie May . . .
'My skin is not like yours' she said 'and my eyes are black, not blue;
Suzie's skin is yellowish, her eyes are different too -
We don't have hair the same colour at all, and we speak in a
different way.
We'll have to have a little chat with the Vicar, this very day.'
So they called on the cleric when school was done, and they queried
their colour and eyes . . .
The Vicar just listened, his eyes full of love, as they asked him their
how's and their why's.
'Don't give it a thought, for you mix very well, don't think that you're
each set apart,
You're each loved the same by your Father in Heaven, He sees not
your looks, but your heart.'
So the three little girls went away full of joy, their little hearts full
to the brim,
Three sisters in Christ, each loved just the same . . . and equally
precious to Him.

D Whiteley

A SECRET SORROW

You get up in the morning and wash your face,
Put on your best smile and show not a trace
Of how you are feeling, deep inside
No-one knows of the tears you have cried.
For something has happened, there's nought
you can do,
And what is the point in you feeling so blue?
You have to keep trying, hold on to your dreams
For nothing is ever as bad as it seems.
Although it is raining and your heart is sad
Remember the good things, and don't feel so bad,
For maybe the sun will shine brighter tomorrow
And you will be able to cope with your sorrow.
So, if you've a secret you find hard to bear,
But you can't tell a soul, for nobody would care
There's someone who'll listen, and always be there
Be patient, for God's love, will answer your prayer.

Loraine H Cox

THE DECISION MADE

Up on the top of Tower Hill
An upright man was standing still,
He didn't feel the cool, cool breeze
Wafting around him at the knees.

On that mountain top he stood,
Over his problems he did brood,
He thought he had done his best,
Had he stood his greatest test?

He carefully the decision made,
Before the light began to fade,
He had achieved mental harmony,
He would accept rank in the 'Army.'

He would do his level best,
The discipline would be a test,
He'd lead and teach by example,
And quote texts from the Holy Bible.

His decision made, he then knelt,
And alone he then His presence felt,
He finished his prayer, and then
He heard an echoing, Amen.

A Wilson

THE TRUTH

He walked the road of palm trees, knowing what was to be his fate.
He stood his ground at trial, the crowd was full of hate.
At Calvary he met two others in the same predicament as he,
One was unrepenting, promising the other paradise with me.
His ordeal eventually over, the dreadful deed was done.
But lo on the third day he proved he was God's son.
All of this Christ did for us to show us of God's love
So we can plan our way through life, with guidance from above.

June Abbott

THE LORD IS HERE

Arise O sun, greet the dawn of day,
He is here, let us pray.
Can't you see Him in the dawnlight?
See He comes with Power and Might!
Hail Him! Greet Him! Lord of the Host;
One with the Father and the Holy Ghost.

He is here, hear His voice in the gentle breeze,
Whispers words of comfort and ease,
Of hope; and sins forgiven,
The powers of Hell riven.
He is here, let our voices raise
In songs of thanks and heartfelt praise.

He is here, beside you He walks;
Listen! As to your heart He talks,
'Come all you who have sorrow,
Who are weary and fearful of tomorrow,
Believe in Me; trust in Me,
My Peace, then I will give to thee.

He is here, in the grandeur of the mountains,
The thundering seas, the babbling brooks the
leaping fountains.
In all the beauty and grandeur of creation.
He is here, loving, caring, the manifestation
Of God made Man, whom Sin crucified
On the cross of Calvary He died,
And on Easter morn He rose again
To bring Hope, banish fear, and pain.
Yes, He is here bringing Love exceeding.
'Come to Me all you labour,
Come, My Peace you will savour.
Take up your cross, follow Me.
My Way leads to Paradise for Eternity.

J P Keenan

LIFE AND DEATH

I am secure
In my eggshell world.
Surrounded by friends
Comfort, warmth and love.
I never doubt
That this will last forever.
Then one day
A blow falls . . .
The eggshell cracks . . .
The precious contents spill.
Shivering and afraid
I try in vain
To pull the broken fragments
Round me.
But my eggshell world is broken
And I, a trembling speck
Am left alone,
Staring through
The jagged splints
Into the deafening silence
Of Time and Space . . .
Into the blinding darkness
Of Eternity.
So this is the end.
In the darkness a hand takes mine . . .
I yield my frailty to its powerful grip.
'Yes. This is the end . . .
But also the great beginning . . .
I planned it so.'

Norah M Field

BACK TO THE DRAWING BOARD

A nestling calls its beak agape,
Its snug home hidden, soft and warm,
Carefully fashioned built to shape,
Ergonomic cup to fit its form.

Young deer dappled freeze in grass -
Striped wild piglet hides from view,
Still and breathless as predators pass.
Silent owl floats hunting shrew.

Reversed world of bats hanging in cave,
Cold world of fishes floating in stream;
Displaying bird of Paradise in colours brave.
Eerie death watch beetle hiding in beam.

The Designer drew and made them all,
Ordered habitat and food;
Created species great and small,
Fashioned all nature and saw it was good.

But feckless Man can cause change,
Conjure deserts out of wood,
And thoughtless greed can re-arrange
The Great Designer's works . . . for good.

Di Bagshawe

YOU HAVE YOUR GOD, I HAVE MINE

You have your God, I have mine
Let's agree to differ on what is divine
We must not interfere with another's belief
So let's not give each other any grief.

When I lift my eyes to the sky
I promise never to ask why
You turn and face towards the east
And touch your head in the dust.

I may think my God is best
And my church better than the rest
But never will I criticise
What seems better in your eyes.

You have every right to pray
To whatever God you say,
And I will show respect and love
And carry peace like a dove.

So join your hands and slow compassion
To all our brethren's religion
For whatever differences they may bring
Your God and mine is the same thing.

Edna D'lima

INTO THE ARMS OF ANGELS

When a loved one from this life departs
they carry the love of many hearts,
into the land that's fit for kings
where the choir of heavenly angels sings.

Down golden pathways hand in hand
through gardens of flowers oh so grand,
into a paradise where evil is banned
finding happiness forever more.

Be not sad they left so young
they carry your love into the sun,
for now life's race they have finally run
they go to claim their prize.

It may be hard to let them go
tears like sparkling jewels may flow,
but in your heart you will come to know
that they have now found peace.

Victor R A Day

A WALK WITH GOD

I feel God's grace within me, His presence all seeing;
As the wind caresses my face, my body, my whole being.
My spirit soars, floats, dances in joy, my soul alive, vibrant
As His loving touch covers me with comfort, contentment.
The brilliant sun, clear blue sky, open pastures, God's creation
Fills my senses with energy, life, awe, wonderful recreation.
Stillness enfolds me, sweet moments of calm, deep inner peace.
Alone, not lonely, the pace of life slows, worries all cease.
Fine gentle breeze, filling me, lifting me higher and higher
With God's power, increasing my faith with strength and fire.
I give myself totally to you, dear Lord, on this earth below,
To do your will safe in your care and the love you bestow.

Live happily in the now.
  Do not fret or worry how,
    Or wonder when, or query what or why,
      Just trust God and your faith will never die.

Esmé E Wilson

ENFOLDED IN LOVE

I took a gold needle,
And a golden thread fine,
Then quietly stitched you,
A blanket Divine,
Each corner embroidered,
With precious sweet care,
And each single stitch,
Brought love, that I share,
I painted a rose,
In the centre or heart,
And its delicate fragrance,
Was yours to impart,
To all of the world,
His beauty to feel,
Then a rainbow of colours,
My blanket revealed,
It was edged with compassion,
And folded with love,
Angels then wrapped you in it,
From Heaven Above,
Trust in your creator,
Each night and each day,
Go quietly within,
Sincerely to pray,
God listens in silence,
With wisdom and care,
Then He folds you in love,
So you know He is there.

Janette Campbell

NEW LIFE

You may feel insignificant despondent
and alone
With no hand to comfort or sanctuary
of home
Take heed you are needed if you know right
from wrong
There's a task laid out for you
Unique to God's great plan

If a privileged few have left no room
in the Inn
You'll find love in the stable where great
things begin
There's Myrrh, Frankincense and Gold
awaiting for you
To be shared together with friends that
are new

Grasp inspiration hold fast to what's good
You'll be tested by fire as pure Gold should.

O Bedford

DIVINE TRUTHS OF INNER PEACE

In perfect peace thou'lt keep him
Whose mind is stayed on thee,
Help us Lord to know this truth,
For knowing sets us free,

Free from fear and worry
And all unrest that brings,
Free with inner peace
So we might soar on wings

Above the fret and fever
Of this earthly life,
To reach a higher realm of peace
Of tranquillity, not strife,

We'll not know peace thro' study,
But from deep within our soul,
Yet prayers will help us find it,
Then seeing, will make us whole,

But once we've grasped this truth,
We'll know it evermore,
That if we keep our minds on Thee,
There's inner peace galore,

For God's within each soul,
His temple there to dwell,
Oh help us Lord to know this truth,
Then all with us is well.

Lola Perks-Hartnell

A NEW PERSPECTIVE

Try out a new perspective,
Find good in all you see,
See the beauty all around you,
Which was made for you and me.
Try enjoying quietness,
A reflecting time alone,
Away from all the noise,
Of a crowded busy home.

Forget just for a while
That your life is run by time,
Have freedom to enjoy your work,
But be sure to draw the line.
Time is of the essence
Is what people tend to say,
But don't let them persuade you
You're the one who's lost the way.

The way to real true happiness
Is accepting who you are,
Begin to love yourself
And then you'll go on far.
So try out a new perspective,
Finding good in all you see,
It will make a great big difference
To the person you will be.

Joanna Drake

REJOICE IN GOD'S GIFTS

Bright glowing colours around us we see,
Birds on the wing and the fish in the sea,
Blossoming flowers, green leaves on the tree,
Great gifts of beauty wherever they be.
All things around God has given us free,
Sent in His love, both to you and to me.

Sounds of the ocean and waves on the shore,
Birds singing sweetly, the lion's loud roar,
Lowing of cattle and sheep as they graze,
Sunshine and showers and bright summer days,
Music of voices raised up in God's praise,
Tell of His wonders in so many ways.

Let us sing loudly in praise of our King,
Spread wide the message salvation can bring.
Share out the joy that our hearts may take wing,
Know that all greatness from Jesus can spring.
Join the rejoicing, now let us all sing,
Jesus our Saviour is Master and King.

E S W

GOD'S GIFT

Joseph and Mary were man and wife
Soon would come a son into their life
Born in a stable laid into a manger
This special baby would be no stranger

He would travel the land and teach God's law
Perform great miracles which many people saw
His healing hands gave the blind sight
The sick cured to everyone's delight

Twelve disciples were chosen to go and preach
Judas's promise to Jesus was soon to breach
Thirty pieces of silver would send Jesus to a cross
Barabbas set free to the crowd Jesus was no loss

A thorny crown nails pierced in hands and feet
He would resurrect and his following would again meet
The love of the Lord in his heart was strong
Knowing after death with God he would be among

S Edmondson

DEAR LORD

Dear God help me
I need you now
You're looking down
On an old sinner
With a troubled brow
How will I face
Another ordeal without you
My Redeemer, my Saviour
The one I turn to
You're my rock on troubled water
The one who cares
Though sometimes dear Lord
I am unaware
Until I need that guidance
You show me the way
To be less selfish and help others
To know and feel a better day
Better for sharing
And knowing it's true
True to yourself and one's beliefs
To know tranquillity
Blessed peace.

Irene Pearce

GROWING OLD

O Lord forgive my wandering ways
My weakness and my sin
Remember I am tired Lord
With all this rush and din

My bones are getting crumbly Lord
My knees are none too great
My eyes are getting dimmer now
I'm like a creaking gate

I can't remember things so good
The scriptures I forget
I can't sing like I used to do
My ways are slow and set

But I want to tell you Father
My heart is just the same
You're as precious as you were
I still revere your name

I might have wrinkles round my neck
And lines upon my chin
But help this longing heart of mine
Some precious soul to win

Lord you can take the weaker things
And make them strong for you
So take my life and mould it Lord
And help me work for you

Bett Maclean

SEARCHING

Heaven is where God is, I know, but what that means to me,
How can I comprehend, with my poor, sin-laden soul?
Yet, there are moments of time when eternity gleams;
Earthly reflections of heaven, my part of his whole;
Dew on a spider's web, clear in the moment of dawn,
Raindrops, as jewels in velvet, held cupped in a rose;
Undaunted courage, the freshness and vigour of youth,
Innocence shown on the face of a child in repose;
Sun-scattered lake waters, dimpled by soft-blowing winds,
Breathing caressingly as they drift gently away;
Moments of peace in the soul-stifling noise of the world,
Curtains of sleep drawn by God at the close of the day;
Melodies waking some harmony, deep in the soul,
Unspoken words when two hearts are in perfect accord;
That greatest soaring of spirit that man can achieve,
When, in a moment, he knows that he meets with his Lord.
All in an instant these vanish, for, if they remained,
I could not bear the perfection of joy that they give;
Unsatisfied, I still long for those joys which I glimpse,
Yet cannot know, until death gives me freedom to live!

Margaret Wensley

TRUTH AND DOUBT

The words that I write are but meaningless dross
About lives that are lived and loves that are lost
What meaning is found in the lines that I write
When my thoughts are confused and lost in the night

How can I say what my heart really feels
When it pounds up and down then falls under heel
I am down at the bottom of life's dreary trough
I am flying in clouds in the sky up above

The torture I feel of not knowing when
I will see you again and perhaps not even then
When I think my life's dream is about to arrive
You take hold of my heart and crush it to size

What more can you give to help me decide
To carry on living in life's great divide
Or seek pastures anew where my heart can be free
Among flowers and grasses in heaven's great see

But only your truth will help me to see
And help me to find where my future can be
Whether living for you with a heart full of love
Or searching for peace like the gentle white dove

Fiona Higgins

THE CHRISTIANS' HOPE

The dead shall rise - we shall be changed
We shall all meet up there in the air
Then we'll descend in that glorious new city
To live with our loved ones there

When the Lord comes back to Zion
To His Holy mountain again
As 'Lord of Lords' and 'King of Kings'
With His saints forever He'll reign

He will come in His Father's glory
Which was His before worlds began
What a wonderful day that will be
- God united with man

No more need of sun or moon
The Lord will be our light
The Lion and the Lamb will lay down together
No more crying - or pain - or night

When the Lord makes up His jewels
Dross He'll cast to the flame
He'll say 'Come beloved of my Father'
And He'll call us by a brand new name

Norah Page

IN TIMES OF SUFFERING, LORD

In our times of suffering, Lord,
Help us to find peace.
In our times of despair, Lord
Help, our restless hearts to cease
From tossing to and fro,
And turning inside out . . .
In our times of suffering, Lord,
Help us never doubt
That you care for us and love us,
And will take us by the hand
If we just call out to you, Lord;
Though we may not understand
Some of the things in life
That we have to go through.
Help us to know, Lord
You stand beside us grieving, too.
In a world that's turned away from you,
Treats you with such destain:
It helps to know one day, Lord,
You will rise, and come again.
There will be an end to suffering,
To sorrow and to war;
Man once more will live, Lord,
By your book of Holy Law.
So help us in our suffering,
To place our burden upon you
For you know all about it, Lord:
Suffering was born in you.
For the sinful world we live in
You've grieved, and played your part;
Lift us above our suffering, Lord,
Give us peace in our hearts.

Martina Peters

THE TRUE WAY

Why search?
For that, which your eyes cannot see!
Why listen?
For that, which has no sound!
You cannot touch
that, which is without form.
Though you may scream, cry, beat your chest and perform acts of devotion,
Bow down, burn candles and worship
You will still be no nearer to the truth.
And you will build Temples and Mosques, Synagogues and Churches,
houses for your Gods to rest.
When, the house is your body!
And there, is where it dwells.
In your image you carve stone and wood to look like you
Yet what you seek is beyond your reach.
The way that can be spoken is not the real way,
the name that can be named is not the real name.
Believe in yourself
and you may find harmony
between what is and what is not!
Those who know do not speak,
those who speak do not know.

Patrick J Cassidy

TODAY - I WAS MOVED

I woke to the sound of the radio
The news was just the same
Tales of war and famine
The killing, winning game.

I made myself some breakfast
Cereal with toast to follow
But the wasted figures on TV
Were a little harder to swallow.

Later setting off to work
I left my conscience behind
The images which had so moved me
Now filed at the back of my mind.

That evening after I'd had dinner
Whilst waiting for a film to start
I wrote out an appeal donation
Happy that I'd played my part.

At night with my head on my pillow
Those pictures in front of me creeped
And although I had done my duty
It was a while before I could sleep.

I tossed and turned in my dreaming
A voice said, 'I've called you apart
Yet Christian you've still to realise
True giving comes from the heart.'

I woke to the sound of the radio
The news was just the same
Tales of war and famine
The killing, winning game.

D A Davis

THE LONG GOOD FRIDAY

'Ever heard of the long Good Friday?'
The radio announcer said,
'A programme of sport, noon till nightfall,
From now till you're ready for bed.'

'Yes, I've heard of the long Good Friday,'
My stricken heart sadly replied,
'When for sport they sat watching dice fall,
While the Saviour hung there and died.'

Men were heedless that long Good Friday
Of earth's darkness, temple veil torn,
But for those who cared, how delightful
The joy of that first Easter morn!

K B Law

READ ON, IF YOU DARE!

A Maker and Sustainer of all creation:
The whole earth, the seas in roughest motion,
Me and all human, little foxes and high hills,
Hands in praise and stubborn wills.

Without Him, nothing is; alive or under sod;
And nothing is, that is not God.
His name is the Great I Am. All existence,
He is Being's essence.

There are three ways this one God may inspire.
I look within myself, and see Him, my fire,
My Sustainer, my Neighbour, my Saviour.
I look out at my neighbour -
Let your heart bleed
For those in need.

I see God
In all learning ad-
-Vances - Einstein's space curled,
And in natural beauty, the natural world;
And in humour, in enjoyment, in the comely
And the unlovely.

I look out at the universe' furthest expansion
And I see nothing but God:
He is incarnate in this odd
Way. But of Him that is only a fraction
And that only touches fringes
He far o'er-reaches.

He is beyond all worlds

And all words -
The greatest energy
And the smallest synergy.
Although in the ultimate smallness
There is nothing there - in all its fullness.

He is the dance : He is the one, pattern, rows,
The design of all things. He chose
To incarnate by number, by equation, by evolution,
By random number, by chance, by coincident motion,
By opposing two forces and the tension
Between them, - three in Balance.

He is rest, the eternal spinning stillness,
The shout, the Voice in the silence.

W A Saxton

GOD IS ALWAYS WITH US

We know you're always with us
Even though we're unaware
That you know our every thought
And hear our every prayer
We know that we can trust you
To help us through our days
To take us gently by our hand
And guide us through life's ways
We know that you'll protect us
From the dangers we may face
And with your patient guidance
We will follow your Christian ways
We know that you truly love us
Because you sent your only son
To die for the sins of humanity
What greater sacrifice

Margaret Fleming

BLESSING

Blessings so wide and abundant
        Come showering down like rain
I look up and then, he thrills me again
        Blessings again and again.

Blessings in care and provision
Blessings in shelter and food
Blessings and praise, filling my days,
Praise to the Lord who is good.

Blessings from friendship and family,
Christian fellowship sweet
Blessing that flow,
From him whom I know,
As I worshipfully sit at his feet.

Blessings from God's holy spirit
That flow down and touch me with love.
Blessing that fill when I'm empty,
        And seeking his grace from above.

Blessings too great for recounting
Blessings from God great and small.
He's forgiving of sin
If I want to bless him
I can do it by giving my all.

J Facchini

A STEP FROM THE CROSSROADS

You can be at the Crossroads
Not knowing which way to turn
When will difficult times be over?
For stillness and peace you yearn

There are feelings of ire and frustration -
Loneliness, unease and fear
But trust and faith can quell the pain
If you listen to the word in your ear

It will come to you if you open your heart
And let God in your life play His part
He is there to comfort and ease the stress
If you talk to Him and your troubles confess

His Power is great, His Power is all
Believe in Him to lift when you fall
Life can be hard and the crossroads unsure
Don't go it alone, it's too hard to endure

Maureen Stewart-Condron

LIFE'S JOURNEY

Life's journey is so wonderful
in our travels every day
sharing those joys and sorrows
meeting new friends on the way.

Though sometimes are quite difficult
we will take them in our stride
when companions faith and hope
are forever by our side.

Dear Lord we pray and trust in you
seeking strength, love and your light
to shine, guide and protect us
along paths both day and night.

Through all the ups and downs of life
grant us patience and your peace
send your spirit gently down
blessings then will never cease.

Margaret Jackson

UNDAUNTED HOPE

Draw me ever closer Lord
For I am old and grey
'Twill not be long, so I have heard,
Till in my grave I lay.
So clothe me round in mercy
Not in a shroud of grey
Forgive, and don't desert me,
Be ever near, I pray.
Yes, I have sinned Lord, all my life,
As you and I both know
Yet still your love shines clear and bright
Now time is running slow.
Enfold me in your loving arms,
A sinner such as I
Keep me safe from all alarms
Dear Lord, and when I die,
Give your angels charge I pray
Until death's sleep be through
Then let me wake on Judgement Day
To always be with you.

Pamela D Harris

ONLY ONE

The Bible says: one faith,
Man has them by the score.
God's word condemns many things
But they, the religions ignore.

Homosexuality heartily condemned,
God's Kingdom they can't inherit,
What's Christendom's stand on this?
It's accepted, and with merit.

The Creator hates a divorcing,
Except in cases of porneia,
How do most churches treat this?
They ignore it, and with good cheer.

They preach good go to Heaven,
Where does it say this is so?
The only place it's mentioned
Says only 144,000 will go.

Paradise was proposed for earth,
This, God will still have done,
If you don't think this is so,
Then eternity, you'll have none.

Raymond J Lewis

IN OUR DEEPEST DESPAIR GOD TRULY IS THERE

O Lord the trial is hard, my strength seems almost but gone,
And I wonder just how much longer can I go on.
But no circumstance can the Christian from Your love sever,
For You have promised to leave nor forsake me never -
Our refuge and strength, present to help amidst life's alarms,
As around and underneath are the everlasting arms.
Thus I draw nigh to you now to call upon Your name,
To plead your precious promises which I in faith claim.
So as I pass through the waters, O Lord stand by me,
And through the raging fire, O preserve me safely.
Make my experience the reality the Apostle Paul knew,
Who had this answer to prayer - 'My grace is sufficient for You.'
So Lord bear me up, with Your help and strength endued,
For I know You work all things together for my good,
As part of Your greater, heavenly design,
My faith to strength, purify and refine.
And Lord, You've told us not to be anxious about anything,
But all our petitions to the throne of grace bring.
For whate'er we ask, believing, we shall receive,
Finding mercy and grace to help in time of need.
So I gladly therefore cast all my care upon You,
Who can exceeding abundantly above all that I ask or think do.
And I thank You, Heavenly Father, for your loving care,
For in our deepest despair You truly are there.

Ian Caughey

SHUTTING THE GATE

How do you cope when all seems lost,
And all you attempt ends in tears?
Do you find more to add to your load,
And nothing works to ease your fears?

One by one the troubles mount up,
But you just can't leave them alone,
You hug them close, gnawing away
Like a dog who won't leave a bone.

It's time to stop and look behind -
You've forgotten to shut the gate;
Too long your past has followed you,
Now let go before it's too late.

So turn around, forget the past,
You will find it's the only way,
You have to learn to shut the gate,
And step forward with Him today.

Mary Care

GOD'S PROMISE

Hating, night and day,
Shutting the world away.
Problems make you blind,
Anger clouds your mind.

All you want to do is weep,
Even cry yourself to sleep.
Blaming God for your strife,
Wishing you could end your life.

Feeling everyone's to blame,
For your heartbreak, pain or shame.
All situations take two,
There's not just me! Just you!

It's easy not to believe,
Our eyes to deceive,
So pray! Pray! Deep from your soul.
Let your faith make you whole.

God's not looking at your sin,
Only the love you have within,
You will not see him until the end,
He'll come,
In the shape of a neighbour or a friend.

We are all free to choose,
Some we win, some we lose,
When the mind clears, and the tears too,
May God's rich love dwell in you.

God did not promise,
Sun with no rain,
Joy with no pain,
Peace with no sorrow,
God did promise,
A better tomorrow.

Tonina Cilia

THE SECRETS OF MY KINGDOM

The secrets of My kingdom
I will impart to you
Gradually, when appropriate
As you go forward to *The new*

Have your total awareness
Fixed upon *My* soul
Then life and all its difficulties
Will not take such a toll

For *I* have enough *love* for all
Spread throughout the land
And *I* will impart gladly
So come on, take *My* hand

Let us go forward together
To learn all that is right for you
To progress joyously on your journey
Doing all that you need to do

For *the secrets of My kingdom*
Will open up to you, a *new world*
Where positivity, joy, love and peace
Is now the banner to be unfurled.

Jade Deacon

THE ONLY WAY

O loving God
If only everyone could turn
And stop the wrangling
Concerning BSE; and LSD.
It was written of our Lord
'Butter and honey shall He eat,'
But we, all of us, have contaminated
The wealth You gave us.
You warned us this would happen
Should we fail to live Your way,
And now the situation is among us,
Yet is seems the small, the great, the ignorant,
The clever and the brilliant
Will not turn around
And live as You command,
The way of purity and peace,
Truthfulness and honesty,
Caring for our families and neighbours,
With care for all the riches that You gave us,
Care for living creatures
And the fertile, fruitful land.
Please renew Your love towards us
With forgiveness and compassion,
And by Your grace give guidance
With a deeper understanding,
Turn us to Your holy word
Our gracious Lord and Saviour,
Teach us to live Your way
And in Your mercy heal us.

Elizabeth Mills

THE CROSS-ROADS OF LIFE

A mixture of feelings; worries and ills,
Sometimes in valleys, sometimes upon hills.
Seeking and searching down road upon road,
Forever carrying our heavy load.

There's many signposts to show the world's ways;
Some of them dreary and some very gay,
All so tempting in a self-centred way.

One day on our journey of trouble and strife,
We all must end up at the cross-roads of life.
There's a fence there to sit on that's bowed with the weight
Of the people who sat there and left it too late!

The road to indifference is very smooth; and it's wide, with
Many places in which to hide.
The verges are sandy; and not too difficult to tread,
But are very useful for burying your head.

The road to religion seems a sure path to take:
Just through the fence with the rather large gate.
Footpaths to heaven each one seems to call,
At the end of each one is a solid brick wall!

The third road is much different, not easy to find
And sometimes it seems like the one left behind.
It's narrow and uphill with dangers to meet,
But the scenery on all sides is breathtaking sweet.

Upon this road you *will* fall down; at times,
Think you are lost, but each stone is marked
With the sign of the cross.
The foundations were laid long before time began . . .
The Lord made this road as part of his plan.

Neville Hawkins

MEANING

Is there any sense in the world today?
As I look around, I see madness and disarray;
It sometimes seems like chaos has taken over again,
That even the shadow of Eden is buried in the grave.

Who rules the hearts of men,
Who rape and cheat and kill?
Is it his own evil nature,
Or the devil striking again?

Can I find any meaning in a world of sorrow and pain?
I wonder in my heart, and see and feel the strain,
The world has gone off the rails as it follows its own way,
Not to the light of heaven, but to somewhere dark and depraved.

The only hope I know is in One outside and above,
Who came to this world in Jesus and gave new direction and love.
He is here among us and around us, if, we'll just stop and think for a while,
Only He can bring peace and direction to draw us from Satan's power.

O, give us Lord, the power, to go fearlessly into the world,
To show by our love and compassion that we've found the way through
the fire.

Chris Murray

COMING OUT

The day I came out of Mum's womb I was labelled a queer,
I liked to play with dolls,
All the other boys had their guns and Action Man gear,
Conditioning sort of changed my ways,
At an older age I was *fancying* girls,
Well anyway that's what I told the boys,

What about secondary school then?
There I became a bit of a loner,
I seemed isolated from the crowd,
I was taunted, beaten up and spat at,
You name the punishment I received it,
Oh how often I wished that school would burn down.

What about Mummy and Daddy then?
Well I never told them until I was 15,
Thank God they were alright,
But they couldn't save me from the outside world,
Whether I liked it or not it was up to me.
All alone I had to be strong and fight for what I believe to be right.

Now I don't pretend
I know myself better than most men ever will,
My faith is so strong within,
It brought me through those very dark times,
When the world seemed so cold and unkind,
It was my God that saw the light.

Carl Bridgman

UNTITLED

Have you heard the quiet voice
Which says, 'Come unto me'?
Jesus knows the feeling
Of your least infirmity.
He has a special care for those
Who labour and are weak.
His heart is with the lowly,
And his blessing on the weak.

He doesn't promise to remove
The burden which you bear,
But he'll be with you, every step,
To take the greater share.
And when you say, 'Your will be done.'
Believing he knows best,
You'll find his yoke is easy,
And his service perfect rest.

Pat Wray

WILL YOU REMEMBER ME?

There once was a man called Jesus,
Who came with a message of peace,
He wanted to show, what we all need to know,
How hatred and evil must cease.
Well most have forgotten Jesus,
The mercy and love of His way,
They have placed their trust in anything else,
They listened not to what He did say.
So now we live in a world gone mad,
Where anxiety and violence abound,
And our companion with us every day,
Is the fear we find all around.
Maybe it's time to remember Jesus,
So our lives can be free of all strife,
To dwell in the love of He who cares,
The way - the truth - and the life.

T A Hall

OPEN ALL HOURS

Like a spaceship it has chambers -
Four to be exact. There are times
When they are not totally intact -
Adversity - winning and losing -
Have a hand in opening
The Tabernacle of Deity.
Life's blood flows through -
Goes in blue, comes out red;
'Spilled for all on the cross.'
They said. 'Do unto others . . . '
Most are all up in the air, but
Those that can see Him who died
Nailed to a tree, our hearts
Are imbued with endless powers -
To remain - *open all hours!*

Mary Devlin

WHERE IS THE LOVE

Where is the love
That this world needs
Fear drives it out
Bringing selfishness and greed

Where is the faith
Keeping fear at bay
Knowing it'll be alright
Keeping despair away

Where is the hope
That keeps driving us on
Against all the obstacles
Keeping us strong

Where is the charity
Letting us care for each other
Knowing we're all equal,
Every person a brother

They're all there inside
Your power and your strength
Ignore the fear, knowing they're there
And you'll triumph in the end

Elizabeth Loy

DOUBLE NOUGHT

For one slender moment
I came to imagine
A fashion transcendent
Attending a future
That lies not so distant:
Instantly new; more
Or less terrifying.
God knows that this turning,
This journey, this dying,
Is more than a capsule
Without our existence,
But some flat insistence
On keeping our faces
Lit up by creation,
Replacing the traces
Of light in our bodies:
A new dose of closeness,
Supposing in God we
Transcend every distance;
Each difference showing -
Instantly nothing
Within this transcendence.
Moved onwards to ever,
Yet sent on together -
Into a space when the
Future lies latent:
For one slender moment.

John Marc Hughes

CHRISTIANITY THE ONLY FAITH FOR ME

Sweet Jesus who loves me greatly,
Proved it by dying for me,
Helps me daily,
Leads us over life's rough sea.

He lives in me, helps me in all things,
Jesus is mine, and I am his,
An encourager, a corrector, my spirit sings,
A wonderful saviour He is.

J A Adams

HEAVEN

I have often wondered as many have before.
About the after life we've heard
behind God's heavenly door.
What happens when we say goodbye
to those we've loved and lost.
What do we know about our souls,
how do we count the cost.
We all have our private thoughts
and wonder who to ask.
But who on this earth can tell us,
it would be a daunting task.
If we have lived a Godly life
and helped others all we could.
If we've enjoyed our years on earth
as God said we should.
Our souls then leave and go to him
for he has called us home.
Go through those shining heavenly gates,
for we've just been on loan.
We say goodbye, and mourn
those who were dear to us.
We try to come to terms and cope
with our distressing loss.
Then God takes us by the hand and
we will understand,
That one day we will also leave and
join his heavenly band.
Our souls to meet with loved ones
who have gone before.
Exalting then with wonder,
stepping through God's heavenly door.

Anne Baker

TO WALK WITH JESUS

I wish I'd walked with Jesus
Two thousand years ago,
And felt His holy presence.
What was He like to know?
This man who's been beside me
Since my first breath of life,
Who's shared with me the good times,
And steered me through the strife.

I wish I'd sat beside Him
And known His gentle touch,
This meek and humble man
Who taught His followers so much.
If eyes full of compassion
Had gazed into my own;
If I could just have told Him
That my heart was His alone.

And yet I still can tell Him,
Each time I kneel to pray,
For He does walk beside me
And sit with me each day.
Yes, Jesus is my master,
My shepherd and my guide,
And when, at last, He takes me home,
In His house I'll abide.

Kay Spurr

ALONE

Curtains moving
Days declining,
Tele boring
Night is calling,
Bed's awaiting
Comfort room,
Blanket on
Electric warm,
Snug, secure
God is here.

Margery Richards

YOU

In my times of trouble
I call on You.
You are the only one
that can help me through
the troubles and strife
in my life.

When I feel all alone
I come to You.
I call on Your name -
You hear,
You answer -
I know you do!

You are the one
that made the heavens
and the earth.
And Your Holy Spirit
fills me
giving me a second birth!

You made me, Lord.
I don't know why.
when I call out Your name
You answer my cry.
When no-one else is there -
there's You!

Roger Hampton

LETTER TO HEAVEN

What is this?
this feeling deep inside me . . .
That fills my soul,
with inner peace.
Is it love?
Yes, and so much more.
You're in my heart,
and in my soul.
You are my life!
You bring me joy!
You blessed our lives,
with Your darling boy.
To all the world . . .
You gave your all.
You lift us up,
each time we fall.
Dear Lord, my Father,
from up above,
I give to You,
my life with love.

Kathleen Sillitto

HEAVEN AND EARTH

My faith in God isn't very strong
To some they think is o so wrong
In the distance a bell does ring
Calling me to come and sing.
Finally arriving at God's house
Everywhere quiet as a mouse
For now I kneel down to pray
Hoping tomorrow will be a better day.

God did make heaven and earth
But did he make me at birth?
By making Eve from a bone
Somehow not being shown.
Plus the animals and the flowers
Most of all, sunshine and showers
What did he put me here for?
I'm sure I don't know anymore.

In heaven and in hell
God knows us very well
There's nowhere for us to hide
For he shall seek and he will find.
In each and every little corner
Even somewhere across the border
For no matter what you say
His presents are with us every day.

Life now has truly begun
And God's work now is done
It's time to take a rest
For all must try and do our best.
This world belongs to you and me
For each and everyone to be free
Maybe one day he will return
Perhaps to hear what you did learn.

Maureen Hyam

UNTITLED

At Easter let us turn our thought
To every deep reflection
On all the havoc we have brought
In many a direction

In cruel war, in famine too
Crass inhumanity
Throughout the earth that sees anew
Our mass insanity

Let us, at this sombre time
Make way for sense to bring
Our deepest thinking to sublime
Thoughts of sweet nature's spring.

Maxwell Bruce

JESUS COME BACK

From what I can remember
From the lessons at school
Jesus was our Saviour
And he was very cool

He came from our creator
In the form of a man
Teaching people God's behaviour
To do the best we can

Oh Jesus come back
To show us all how
Jesus come back
'Cos we need you now

Although I hardly ever pray
I think of you so often
I dream and hope about the day
You're here again with every nation

You made us a promise
To return to earth again
I'll hang on to that promise
And hope it's soon again

Oh Jesus come back
And knock on every door
Jesus come back
We need you so much more

Peggy Ruth Banks

AWAKENED

It woke me with its singing -
The voice was loud and clear,
I thought of all my family
And all I hold most dear.

My eyes were opening and so
Another day had dawned.
I wanted to be positive
But many times I yawned.

I gave the day to God above
And asked that I'd have joy -
Joy amidst whatever came -
Sad thoughts He would destroy.

So I could be more helpful
I also asked for grace
So I could be more tolerant
And speak with smiling face.

I then arose to face the day
After talk and prayers.
I heard the melody of the birds
As I went down the stairs.

'Your will today not mine my Lord.
I will trust You and obey -
Then everything that I do effect
Will make a lovely day.'

Pat Melbourn

THE BAPTISM

In the wilderness of Judea
Came John the Baptist to baptise
His disciples came from far and near
The learned men and the wise

Now John wore a garment of camel's hair
Around his waist was a girdle of leather
Wild honey and locusts were his fare
As he sheltered in the hills from the weather

John baptised in the Jordan river
The waters were muddy and shallow
One day it was Jesus who came hither
And was baptised on the east-side in a hollow

With his fellow Galilleans Jesus journeyed south
To where John was preaching to a crowd
John talked with priests who asked by word of mouth
They were getting impatient and shouted rather loud

'We would like to know just who you are.'
John replied 'I am not the Messiah.'
'Well, do you come from afar?'
'No, and neither am I Elijah!'

'There is One who is greater than I
Who will come and give you sight
I am not worthy His sandals to untie
The Son of God - the world of light.'

You must believe in Him for eternal life
He has everything in His power
Amidst the trouble and the strife
He can be your leaning tower.

Pauline B J Smith

FROST BITE

I saw the tree in the winter's sun, saw new life already begun.
Fat buds, brown and ready to break when balmy spring bid them awake.

I saw the tree in its leafy dress blossoming pink for fruitfulness.
A sudden wind blew icy cold, such fragile wings could not unfold.

I saw the tree as summer flew, no mellow fruit on branches grew
Promises of springtime gone, and the cold north wind blew on.

I saw the tree in the winter's sun, saw new life had again begun.
I said to God a silent prayer, 'Next autumn let the fruit be there.'

I entered the church one Sunday morn as parents gave thanks for a child new born.
I felt the promise of such joy that could embody that little boy.

I entered a school one summer day and saw that little child at play.
His eyes were clear as bluest skies as happy hours went ticking by.

I saw the child become a youth, no-one told him the holy truth
He had no rod to lean upon, it was so easy to go wrong.

I saw the youth become a man, but I didn't see when sin began
For it grew so slowly day by day from the moment he first learned to play.

I entered the church one Sunday night, his parents knelt in sorry plight.
They had not taught their child to pray. They did not know the words to say.

I saw them kneeling side by side, tear streaked cheeks they could not hide.
'We did not know he took cocaine,' over and over they said it again.

I entered the church one Friday past, the final curtain, the final act.
I placed my flowers on his grave, I prayed my Lord his soul to save.

I entered the church on Sunday morn to praises for a child new born.
Oh! Heavenly Saviour in your arm shelter him from any harm.

His father died from lack of faith, he never knew your love and grace.
As the flower turns to fruit let no evil seed take root.

Touch his mother, let her know the way to teach her child to grow.
Show her Kind Shepherd, holy truth, then Satan cannot steal his youth.

Fran Vincent

THE MANIFEST

So hot and sultry, I could not sleep,
Long before the dawn had broken,
When in the silence, before the twilight,
I thought I heard a voice so softly
Spoken;
'Please come with me to the city wall,'

I donned attire, I walked outside,
I slowly wandered towards the wall;
All the while I listened to this
Whisper soft, like an angel's call;
As I stood before the city wall.

This angel's voice in quietude, like
God's command: To stand quite still;
To see a loved-one come into view.
I gazed in silence upon the wall;
She held my hand.

Then through the wall, *the manifest*,
It was my loved-one in heavenly
Raiment;
My heart was pounding within my breast.
I looked upon her lovely face,
Saw the love within her yes, she
Moved towards me with heavenly grace.

She spoke to me, 'I love you still,'
As I shall do forever-more:
Will always be, here beside you,
For when you call;
I'll cherish you by this city wall.

George Ponting

IT'S NOT FAIR GOD

It's not fair God.
Babies dying,
Mothers crying.
It's not fair.

It's not fair God.
People with no hope
Unable to cope.
It's not fair.

It's not fair God.
People living on the street
With nothing to eat.
It's not fair.

It's not fair God.
When we won't hear their cry,
When we won't even try
To help them
It's not fair.

Malcolm Lisle

FAITHFUL SERVANT

Faithful, waiting for Messiah,
no thought of his life starting in her womb.
'How can this be?' - it defies all reason.
Yet here begins the holy season.

> And in the simplicity of her mind,
> defying logic, her faith is profound.

Waiting on the angel's words,
thoughts of her own life die in her heart.
'May it be just as you say'
and with these words, gives her life away.

> And through this selfless human heart
> God's new humanity has a start.

Expecting pain, hurt, rejection,
the cost is great to her mortal frame.
'A sword will also pierce your soul'
but what you grieve makes humanity whole.

> And in her weary body's labour
> she knows that she bears God's favour.

Tim Ford

THE PROMISED LAND

There is a land where I can go
'tis the promise given to me.
'Tis full of love and laughter
where tears just cannot be.

The sun will keep on shining
no clouds will be in the way.
This land I call Foreverland
for forever there I'll stay.

All things of earth forgotten
all the crying and the sighs.
There is no need for either
once beyond earth's mix of skies.

There will be no change of weather
'twill the same always remain.
It is far beyond the rainbow
and far beyond the rain.

My passage is my Saviour the promise is the Word -
He is the beginning of Foreverland
when once the Word is heard.

Alleluia . . .

Rosie Hues

GOD'S CREATION

God Almighty
Knew what He created
in the land, the sky, the sea
He gave us all a magnificent
playground
To enjoy in the land, the sea, the air
His great wisdom was for sure
He gave us day then night
The sun, the moon, the stars
Then He was so clever
He divided the land for us
From the deep blue sea
He put vast countryside
Before us to show His work
of art
To make us think of His
creation
He did so much for
humanity
He gave us pets
such faithful friends
on the scene he put
animals in wild life
Most of all He gave
us a free will
and a wisdom to choose.
God's creation gave so
much to humanity.

Maureen Archibold

FOR PALM SUNDAY

Olive branches on the ground
No holier place around
Jesus came to this place
To fill us with His love and grace

Setting captives free
So we can come to thee
Salvation abounds
O what love we have found

Linda Plummer

FREE

Set free of sin and shame
By Jesus Christ the Messiah
The true King of Israel.

Set free of evil
And this wicked world;
Set apart for the Father!

Set free by Jesus
To worship God!
Set free by the truth . . .

Free to love the Son
Free to receive His Spirit;
Free to preach the gospel!

Ilan Micah Block

JESUS LIVE WITHIN MY HEART

Jesus
live within my heart,
bind me closer, never to part.

Jesus
guide me, let me know,
just how much Your love can grow.

Jesus
Shepherd of Your lamb,
show me just how precious I am.

Jesus
fill me with Your love divine,
let your fingers with mine entwine.

Jesus
Your spirit now lives in me,
fill me to overflowing for others to see.

Jesus
the glory and the praise are all Thine,
help me in this dark world to shine.

Margi Hughes

I WILL REFRESH YOU

In our world of troubles and cares - where can we
turn to bring relief to our sick minds - can we turn
to man for all the answers and concerns - or can we turn
to the hands we can't see - what guidelines do we have -
for our troubled minds - can we do better than turn to the
teachings of the Master Christ - he taught with tender love and
said - come to me you ones that are loaded down - loaded
down with the concerns of this modern world and way of
life - like a mother hen Christ will gather us under his wings -
now in a stronger frame of mind - the Master tells me -
to help others poorer than myself - and when I do the hand
of God will be working with my mind and heart.

R Scannell

PROUD VICTORY WON

Jesus beloved Saviour
Forgive me, Lord, forgive me
You died alone forsaken
My place in hell you'd taken
To honour your mortal suffering
My life and my soul I'm offering
I long to be
At last with Thee
And know Your forgiving grace
My heart is Thine
My King divine
Until we meet face to face.

The shame of the cross on Calvary
Where Jesus knew mortal agony
That I may be forgiven
And earn a bright place in heaven
I thank Thee, dear Lord, I thank Thee
Salvation thus has gained me
Proud victory won
By God's own son
Promised I knew eternity
Proud victory won
By God's own son
To prove God's great love for me.

Mary Poynton

A SONG BEYOND THE GREAT DIVIDE

The gentle breeze stirs through the trees
Caressing aching brows and tearful eyes
From sun-drenched isles and snow clad peaks
The deep blue sky surrounds the world
The dark clouds gather, they all disperse
The morning glory, a new day unfurled.
Fresh air we breathe, new hope revealed.
The great expansion over the land
To penetrate the great divide.
The realisation of someone beyond.
A stretching hand to all mankind.
Arms open wide the aching world
The days and nights so full of crime.
The conflicts of the passing days.
There's a feeling of peace in the great divide;
One sunshine across the whole of the world
One moon sails by in heavenly guide
Spreading fluffy white clouds all entwined,
Reaching over all in the great divide
Chequered patterns of sunlight between the trees
Enchantment of fragrance down country lanes
Raised hearts to heaven on bended knee
A yearning, that takes away your pain
To loving arms that embrace the world,
Extending over all, in the great divide.

Blanche Naughton

SPRING

The day is warm and hazy,
Heat rising from the warm earth.
Spring is just around the corner,
Like a new beginning, a new birth.

The trees shake off their dark winter coats,
Replacing them with new spring gowns.
The frilly white, and pretty pink blossom,
looks far better than the greys and browns.

Now the little bulbs beneath the ground listen,
To all the excitement going on up above.
Then they gently push their way through the earth,
Joining in the laughter, the warmth and the love.

The birds join in the spring chorus,
As they swoop and dive in the warm air.
It's almost a taste of heaven,
Like the wing of a whispered prayer.

The meadows are so lush and green,
With the hedgerows thick with May.
The cuckoo is singing his favourite song,
Wishing he had more time to stay.

The little brook gurgles with laughter,
As it twists and turns round the bend.
Lapping gently over the boulders,
Whispering, 'Spring is the beginning not the end.'

So as I lean on the gate in the meadow,
My heart feels it just wants to sing.
To thank, my God, the creator,
As I gaze on the wonders of spring.

Cassandra Bailey

THE PROPHETS

The time was now near when it must be made clear
exactly it was that God needed.
It was the prophets God chose to do this job.
For Israel's sake, let's hope they succeeded.

Amos was concerned that man's attitude was right to God and also to man.
Hosea spoke of God's love as no other did or can.
Isaiah it was, saw the splendour of God in the very most holy of places.
Jeremiah warned the people repent and reform and was responsible for many long faces

Yes, there was a young prophet called Amos
who worked himself up in a tiswas.
He said love your brother and that means each other.
What a nice man he was, yes he was.

Then there was another young prophet called Hosea.
All the people said, 'We got a right one 'ere.'
He proclaimed God's love which comes from above
and was remembered for many a year.

The next was a prophet called Isaiah
The people he tried to inspire.
As in the temple he trod, he saw a vision of God
rising higher and higher and higher.

Finally there was a young prophet called Jeremiah
who foretold of a future Messiah.
He spoke of a God without any vice
but the people said, 'You are a liar, Jeremiah!'

Harry Wheatley

CREATION

Silence - then a person shuffles slowly past
Silence - a car lazily passes
The sky is a mixture of colours - a tapestry of blues and greys
A bird is perched on a tree top whistling sweetly - silence
Flowers dance in the breeze - magically
The sun is shining and scatters a soft and glorious light upon the countryside
I can see fields - they seem never-ending
Like a patchwork quilt of colour - amazing
A few farm animals graze, the sheep protect their young
The innocent faces of lambs - delight
Houses spoil the scenery - but they are few
Children laughing, enjoying their play
I watch the trees move - each leaf unique
Each shaking rhythmically with the soft wind
Each has been crafted originally - amazing
I smell freshly cut grass - a sign of growth
Silence - it seems as though the earth has stopped spinning and creation has stood still
Creation is beautiful - I am surrounded by wondrous achievements
I stop, I smile
Silence - I stand in awe of creation

Emma Johnstone

FORGIVEN SINS

Nailed to a cross
and left to die,
for all to see
who passes by.
Upon his head,
a bloody crown
made out of thorns,
his head bowed down.
He raised his face
into the rain.
Forgive them Lord
for all his pain.
Hence, on that cross
died Jesus Christ
who gave up his
to give us life.

Scott Cooper

MAY 1944

It was in the month of May 1944
When heaven seemed to open up its golden door
It was in the fifth year of the war.

And on that particular night when the siren blew
A vision came to quite a few.
And looking up into the sky
Behold I saw a crucifix on which the Christ did die.

I wonder what its meaning was
And so did many more.
Maybe it was telling us
That Jesus Christ is coming on this earth once more.

Amy Barrett

STREAMS IN THE DESERT

Streams in the desert shall there be
And flowers in the wilderness.
The singing sands shout joyfully:
Prepare the path of holiness!

The tired hands shall strength receive
And those discouraged edify.
When in God's power they believe,
As does the wasteland beautify.

The blind will see, the deaf will hear.
The mute their silent ways forsake.
As in the desert, streams appear
And burning sand becomes a lake.

A highway shall be crafted there,
On which the Lords redeemed shall make
Their joyous, happy march to where
Their place beside the Lord they take.

Andrew Jones

DON'T LOCK THE DOORS

Don't lock the doors of my father's house
Where else could I go
To shed the tears of a broken heart
A heart so full of woe.

Don't lock the doors of my father's house
For this I strongly pray
The people need it more than ever
I need it day by day.

Don't lock the doors of my father's house
To protect it we must strive
Don't let evil win the day
Let's keep the church alive.

Don't lock the doors of our lovely church
A place where you can go
Away from all the maddening crowd
The only place I know
Where silence reigns
And peace abounds
So please
Don't lock the door.

So now you know just what to do
If you still want this pleasure
Just stay in church
Till the next one comes
And the doors stay open
Forever.

E Willcock

BELIEVE

God has no favourites in religion
in his eyes we are all the same
he only asks us to love him
and believe in his blessed name

each religion has an order of service
in their eyes the one that is right
believe in him in your own heart
and you will be right in his sight

follow the code of compassion
kindness love and belief
and when you reap the fruit of reward
it will be a golden sheaf

in this world the souls are many
in his eyes they are all the same
God he will accept them
if they believe in his name

Frank Scott

THE QUESTION

And for why, what is it you need to know
Is it the path to follow, or just the seed to sow?
And if perchance, the sun should fail to shine,
Do you not know, the way to the light is His Word,
The Word He came to show, by means of His Life
Is the glory of Love and Wisdom and All Power.

Because if the way we would have it
If it didn't clearly shine, radiate the essence of His name,
Wouldn't be the true reflection of His Glory the same,
The same that all peoples' cross the centuries know,
Beats to the same triumphant resound.

Is it only for why, that all you need is to know
Is it when or what or how the reason alone?
What was the harvest or prize He came to show
In the price He had to pay, for the guilty to atone!

Does it really matter, what's the reason for?
To give the answer, to all and every question,
And for why, what is it you need to know?
Is it which path to follow, or what seed to sow?

John Atherton

THE FAMILY TREE

When my life has ebbed away
And suddenly it's *Judgement Day*,
I hope I've made some contribution
To go towards my retribution.

Perhaps a thing I've done or said
Will live long after I am dead,
To make the *world* a better place
Or disappear without a trace.

Just like the tree that's lived its span,
Returned to dust where life began.
So when I'm gone, don't cry for me,
I have *descendants,* like the tree.

And through our children *life goes on*,
Even when, we are dead and gone.

Norman Watson

YOU ARE THE LIGHT

You are the light
In a world of pain,
You are the guide
To show us the way.

You are the hope
In a world of sin,
You help us to cope
When we're about to give in.

You are the power
In a world of need,
You are the food
On which we feed.

You are the glory
Your kingdom divine,
You fill us with awe
You are so sublime.

T S Norman

BESIDE ME

I imagine the waves beating,
moving
inwards and then out.

I see the rising of the sun
within my hands,
and the mist in the horizon lifts.
The sky clears into a cluster of topaz
and in the sea's emerald reflection,
I can hear you breathing.
I can feel you right beside me.

Margaret Reed

ONCE I HAD GOLD

Once I had gold, once I had silver.
Soft silky ribbons to tie up my hair.
Gems from the mountains, pearls from the ocean.
Wealth beyond measure which I would not share.

I had a carriage, a team of fine horses,
Trotting so proudly, they held their heads high,
Dresses of satin, shoes of soft leather,
White silken sheets on the bed where I lie.

Alone I drank wine from fine crystal glasses,
Looking at life from my ivory tower
My heart was so heavy, my soul felt so empty,
Where was the joy in my riches and power?

A camel can't pass through the eye of a needle,
A rich man can't enter God's kingdom above,
Silver can't pay for the blood of the saviour,
And gold cannot purchase so precious a love.

Nothing have I, my wealth now abandoned,
A staff in my hand, and the shoes on my feet.
The grace of my god, and the strength of His spirit
And the love of my saviour makes my life complete.

Luke 18 v 24 - 26

Angie Lakin

WALKING WITH GOD

It's better to walk with God
Than to walk alone,
To have a song upon your lips
Instead a perpetual moan.
Better to enhance your life
With beauty so created,
Than walk through clouds of darkness
That you yourself invented.

Irene Faulkes

A SONNET - THINKING ABOUT PRAYER

Please think! Is thought synonymous with prayer?
It must be so. What other do we need
Than human brain, devoid of any creed,
To free the world of countless cries for care?
Plans flow by fax. From Internet we tear
Fresh interests. We seek to grasp the seed
Of life itself. We search from each new lead
With thoughts we proudly own . . .so bravely dare!

Courageously we strain at drought, disease,
Pollution, politics and peace. We seize
Success at times. Martyrs and heroes die
With willing grace! But do we really try
That simple guidance we are loath to share
By thinking . . .with the listening ear of prayer.

Beryl Dunning

CONSIDER YOUR SHADOW

Consider your shadow.
Have you ever stopped to think,
When the sun comes up before you
And causes you to blink?
Of that other person who always follows you around,
Your constant companion behind you on the ground.

And when the sun's behind you
Your shadow you can see,
A perfect reproduction
A silhouette of you and me.
Your shadow is a faithful friend, a pal who's always there,
Everyone has got one so no one needs to share.

Me and my shadow
Go everywhere together,
Come rain or shine or wind or snow
Come any kind of weather.
My shadow's very personal, in fact he's got a name.
I've called my shadow Jesus, the son of God, the very same.

I know He's always with me
And He never leaves my side.
For He said, "I'm always with you,
Your supporter and your guide".
So when next the sun does shine on you this poem please recall
For I'd just like to ask you, what's your shadow called?

Sue Rose

IONA

There's a charm that belongs to Iona
a beauty of its own.
Colours blended together artists have never shown
These are fashioned by God's own hand, there's
beauty for all to see
If in your mind you would see this treasure
come to the isle with me
Be my companion on the shore, leave the
busy town.
Hear the gulls cry out loud, see them gliding down
The dancing waves make their own song
as they beat about the rocks
The sheep that graze in the meadows
look so bright in their clean white smocks
Now as the day comes to its close, the sky
is glowing and red
The fleecy clouds go drifting by as the
sun goes down to its bed.
The peace I found on this island was
something I've wanted to share
And I thanked God for its beauty that night
when I said a prayer.

Lena Baker

TRINITY PURE AND SIMPLE

Dear Lord can you explain to me,
The mystery of the trinity,
at times it has me quite perplexed.
Though it's clear I'm told in scripture's text.

I always thought that God was one,
Until you sent your only son.
But as I read your scriptures more,
I see your son was there before.

Before you made your great creation,
Earth, sun and stars in strict relation,
Jesus your son was there with you.
So yes, I see that you are two.

There's God the father, God the son,
But God the spirit, three in one?
I find this hard to comprehend,
can scripture help me to this end?

In scriptures old I tried to find,
Explanations of a simple kind
But when I came to scriptures new
Whole new vistas came to view.

Lord Jesus said before he left.
Don't mourn for me you're not bereft.
The comforter will take my place,
To guard and guide the human race.

At Pentecost the spirit came.
Empowering all in Jesus' name,
Enabling faith that does not wane.
To heal, cast out, make whole again.

So thank you Lord that now I know,
That scripture answers us below.
And thus the oneness of the three,
comes through in stark reality.

J E Ryan

THANK YOU LORD

The wonder of this earth,
The wonder of our being,
The wonder of the creatures,
The wonder of eyes so seeing.

The beauty that's within us,
The beauty that surrounds,
The beauty of a new life,
The beauty that abounds.

The miracles that happen,
The miracles that we see,
The miracles that we pray for,
The miracle of you and me.

The faith we feel inside,
The faith of others too,
The faith that keeps us going,
The faith we have in you.

Lord thank you for these treasures,
Lord thank you for your care,
Lord thank you for our being,
Lord thank you for being there . . .

Stella Powell

A LOVE THAT'S RULED BY TIME

You wake up in the morning,
And jump straight out of bed,
You go and take a shower,
To wash your weary head.

You've got no time to listen,
To things I have to say,
You're always in a hurry,
And must be on your way.

Each day we get no younger,
The hour clock ticks on by,
Inside my heart is breaking,
That's why you see me cry.

My love, I'll now explain to you,
what life is all about,
It's caring and compassion,
Not to scream and shout.

Our souls are always searching,
To quench our heart's desire,
No silver, gold or money,
Will doubt my burning fire.

The answer it is simple,
If only you could see,
The greatest gift of all my dear,
Is love and it is free.

So let this be a lesson,
To all who are involved,
Do not take love for granted,
It's worth its weight in gold.

Lyn Peckover

HARVEST PRAISE

Praise ye the Lord,
Praise his holy name alway
For gifts in bright array around us strewn.
For his unchanging love higher than heaven above,
Given to sinners all in Christ his son.
Take thought but for today, seek ye first my way,
All the needed things unto you, my child
I will of my love bestow,
I will bestow.

Richard Taylor

MOONLIGHT

Restless in bed and half-asleep
I stared into the blackened night
Hoping for a star to leap
And fill the heavens with its light.

Slowly through the murky gloom
A silver sheen was spreading wide
Filtering into my room
Searching for a place to hide.

In the sky I spied a ball
Gleaming white and moving slow
Across my window to enthral
With the beauty of its glow.

How can it be this wondrous sphere
Should fascinate me at this time
When each month it does appear
Yet is never deemed sublime.

Gently it fell towards the earth
And left behind some brightening stars
White hot embers giving birth
To thoughts of Venus and of Mars.

Do our neighbours share this sight
Orchestrated by God's hand
Or are their visions in the night
Unspectacular and bland.

My thoughts surrendered to the call
Of sleep asylum for the mind
Eyes softly closed contented all
With moon's gift to all mankind.

Ronald Chantry

THE ETERNAL SHEPHERD

When the road is so long
And the hill is so steep
When the river's so wide
And the ocean so deep
There's a trusting friend who is always there
He will carry you through your deepest despair

When the future's uncertain
As to where you should be
Just look to the saviour
He'll hear your plea
He'll be your protector, your comforting friend
The eternal shepherd who guides to the end

For he died on a cross
Many years ago
To save lost sinners
From eternal woe
And he knows your future, for your life he has planned
Your worries and grief he does understand

So turn to the saviour
On Calvary's tree
He hung there and suffered
For you and for me
In Him you will find everlasting joy
The eternal promise, none can destroy

Wendy Harris

LOOKING ABOVE FOR TRUE LOVE

Creamy white blossoms of perfume fresh
Taste mild but also brings a smile to her
Who tries really hard
But finds it difficult to fight for what is right.
Short in height and legs,
Strong in character and friendship.
She beats the rest because she understands
Humanly the best.
But cannot seem to soar in height to the heavenly light.
Her legs crumble and fall under all the mental toil,
She takes encouragement and prays for the day,
When her mental legs are strengthened by above
When she can climb higher and higher to join with the
Heavenly choir.
This is what she ought to aspire to be a queen is what
God wants in his desire.
The bride and groom will meet face to face floating on
Wings that burn with intense fire,
A burning passion not of lust or human desire,
Only to love who love you first is the song of the heavenly
Choir.
Oh what a delight!
To be at the wedding feast with Christ who with
Creamy white blossoms of perfume fresh
Taste mild but also brings a smile to her
Who tires really hard
But finds it difficult to fight for what is right.

Ian Robinson

ODE TO A YOUNG MOTHER OR THE RAINBOW

'Tis easy to be saint-like if you have no cares.
No worries like the falling pound,
Or where the money for the next bill is coming from.
True, we don't starve here in England or anything dreadful like that;
No earthquakes or tornadoes - but we have our own worries.
Should we be happy-go-lucky?
Ignoring the depression and live it up instead?
Rome was like that before it fell, they say.
I was carefree once.
Free to daydream and do what I liked.
Pretty good I thought.
Then along came a marriage and a demanding son,
Who tries my patience no end.
I had none to start with!
Should we be mindful of the gloom and pain around us?
And do our best to help?
If so, we will get weary and downhearted as we are only human.
So, please, God,
Understand us.
We ask for no reward, or the crock of gold;
Only the rainbow.

M S Bell

TRUST IN GOD

God is loving, God is kind
If you believe in him you will find
It is him you can turn to
In times of trouble and strife
He will understand and help in your plight

He will guide you to waters calm
and watch over you, keep you from harm
His unseen presence is always near
Never worry, never fear

His loving arms enfold us all
If we answer to his call
Do what is right, and just and true
God will comfort and see you through

To a better future full of promise and hope
To enable you to be happy and cope
With what will happen, obstacles to overcome
Kneel at God's feet, thy will be done

D M Brown

AWAKENED BY THE SPIRIT

How inspiring, the spirit of Your love.
When, finally we know
Our need, You will bestow
The greatest gift, sent from our God above.

Such beauty to see, now eyes are open.
Your holy words we read.
The truth then let us heed,
Within our heart received, as bespoken.

Let us nurture love for all as You did.
Act with kindness, always
Rememb'ring all our days
To do Thy will. And evil we'll be rid.

J G Ryder

TONGUES OF FIRE

Sometimes people's tongues can be tongues of fire,
And drag people down into the mire.
But life is too short to be so cruel,
So let us try not to add to the fuel.
What we should do is try to be kind,
Then we will find we have a clear mind.
If we drag people down when they need sympathy,
We are degrading ourselves you must agree.

We should bring sunshine not tongues of fire,
For that is what most people admire.
It can be easy to do things wrong,
But what a relief when a friend comes along.
And offers to help you put things right,
It would make your future look more bright,
To use their tongue in the right direction
Will prove that a friend has shown affection.

For no one knows when they may need a friend,
Or what is lurking around the bend.
For tongues of fire can curl and lick,
To get out of the way, you must be quick.
So let us show our friendly ways,
By that we will show, that kindness pays.

Horace French

TO THE LORD OF THE ARK

Whilst being in this here ark of thine
Life me sometimes thinks can be ever O so dark
and yet sought not I to make homage within
until, thou didst give me the call.
Come, come, come from the dark
for all that lies within is light and life.

Yet speaks me,
Hearken unto my cry O Lord of the ark
for winds of trial come to sift me from within
and troubled waters flood my soul with words of resign, resign
yet my heart says of thee, abide, abide in this here ark of thine.

So to the Lord of the ark I pray,
with words I will to stay,
and yet knowing not what comest may.
But thou hast given thy written word
to all who come to stay, I will in no wise cast out
yet me still hears the serpent's doubts.

O Lord of the ark, I try to pray
but comes to me this new day.
Tears of pain that seems like drops of rain
and fill my heart that I cannot start,
but thou hast said, watch and pray,
for this will keep the devil at bay.

Continually I cry to the Lord of the ark
Why O why can't this pain be gone
yet He did reply, my son, my son, all is not done
in this here ark of mine
So be at peace He speaks, for all one day will come to cease,
says the Lord of ark.

Jim Shanks

BE BOLD, BE STRONG, FOR THE LORD YOUR GOD IS WITH YOU

Nail your colours to the mast and do not budge an inch,
Wield the hammer, make it fast and from it never flinch,
Don't heed the folk who mock you for the things you say and do,
You know that to your God and to yourself you must be true.

Ignore the folk who ridicule and treat you with contempt,
They seem to think that from the laws of God they are exempt,
If they can get you to renounce commitment to the Lord,
They'll jeer and cheer and sneer at you because you broke your word.

Watching every move you make hoping for a tumble,
Just one slip or slight mistake they're happy when you stumble,
"We knew it wouldn't last," they'll say, "he couldn't be a saint,
These Christians are hilarious and most of them are quaint".

Quick to point the finger at the servants of the Lord,
They'll charge you with hypocrisy and speak with one accord,
Your name and reputation will be trampled in the dirt,
You'll face humiliation and your feelings will be hurt.

Remember Jesus told you to expect this kind of thing,
So let his arms enfold you and let your spirit sing.

Mary G Kane

INFORMATION

We hope you have enjoyed reading this book - and that you will continue to enjoy it in the coming years.

If you like reading and writing poetry drop us a line, or give us a call, and we'll send you a free information pack.

Write to

Triumph House Information
1-2 Wainman Road
Woodston
Peterborough
PE2 7BU